My Journey
as a
TEACHER,
MENTOR,
and COACH

My Journey

as a

TEACHER,
MENTOR,
and COACH

I was Never That Clever!

CHRISTINE A PRICE

Library of Congress Control Number: 2013912573
ISBN: Hardcover   978-1-4836-6553-5
               Softcover   978-1-4836-6552-8
               Ebook   978-1-4836-6554-2

I would like to state that at no time, whilst telling my story, have I set out to offend any person(s) or organisation(s) that may have been mentioned and where humour has been used.

This book was printed in the United States of America.

Rev. date: 10/01/2013

To order additional copies of this book, contact:
Xlibris LLC
0-800-056-3182
www.xlibrispublishing.co.uk
Orders@xlibrispublishing.co.uk
305549

Contents

Acknowledgements

I would like to thank my mum and dad for teaching me good values and making me who I am and also my husband and soul mate, Mark, for always being there for me, giving unconditional love, support, and encouragement for me to get where I am today.

In Memory Of

My dear friend and mentor Ruth Rex, who sadly lost her battle against illness before I had a chance to thank her for her support and encouragement and for inspiring me to be like her.

Also, Ian Karten MBE, a true gentleman, who influenced and inspired me during the time I was privileged to work with him as a member of the Karten Network.

www.karten-network.org.uk

Dedicated To

Nick Sanders, my friendly Ofsted inspector, who is truly inspirational and dedicated to improving the learning experience for the learner. He gave me the opportunity to learn so very much. He changed my life through mentoring and coaching me for which I will be forever indebted to him.

Introduction

This book has been written to inspire those considering a career in teaching, those in initial teacher training, and those already in teaching who want to develop existing skills further and find out about new models, ideas, and resources to use. Anyone who reads this book will learn new ways to engage learners in active learning whilst also having fun! Included in the book are examples of effective and innovative practices and insights for a range of audiences.

This book tells the story of Christine's personal journey and the route she took into teaching. She wanted to become a teacher at a very early age, but she might not have achieved all what she has today, through determination and hard work, had she listened to those who told her she wasn't that clever.

The moral of this story is that you should always follow your dreams and if you believe in yourself, you can succeed.

Even those who have been in teaching for a number of years can benefit from reading this book as it shares good practices and mentions different techniques, resources, pedagogical approaches, and models which all help to create an engaging learning environment.

Coaching is a skill that anyone can learn, and it is really useful to find solutions, resolve issues, and improve situations. Action research has identified that 'active learning' is an excellent way of learning and using 'assessment for learning' is an effective way of checking that learning has taken place.

Inspired

Throughout my life I have been inspired
By certain people whom I have admired
Mentors, consultants, and family too
Ruth, Geoff, and Val to mention a few
Ian Karten was a gentleman through and through
Helping lots of disabled people was his mission; it is true
A very kind gentleman always in my mind
No better person could you find
Aunty Dot was a teacher
Who developed many a student
With qualities I could only dream of
Her judgements were always prudent
I wanted to follow in her footsteps
And become a teacher also
The more I learnt from her over the years
Encouraged me even more so
Uncle Bill was a lecturer
In civil engineering
Working in England and abroad
He wrote a book with meaning
Reinforced concrete was what the book was about
Not one page could I figure out
Except that is for the page of dedication
Anything else and I would need an explanation
Meeting Nick would change my life
Like when I met Mark and became his wife
Then came Dawn who inspired me too
To become a consultant and seek opportunities new
So now I want to share my journey with you
And I hope that I can inspire you too!

Chapter 1

Before Teaching

When I was sitting at the usual desk during my maths lesson, working through my SMP book, little did I realise that one day, I would be able to identify just how those lessons had a very negative impact on me.

Previously, I had been put in Set Two, and I used to love my maths lessons as my best way of learning was by seeing a demonstration and then practising myself. The teacher used to give a clear exposition of each topic we covered, followed by a demonstration on the board, and then we would work through exercises before undertaking a 'test' to assess our learning. Nowadays, we would not mention test but instead would call it a quiz so as not to frighten students. I constantly achieved full marks, and because I did so well, I was moved into the top set to work towards the GCE 'O' level exam. Admittedly, I did miss quite a few lessons when I had to go to hospital to have my tonsils removed. That was a story in itself as I was informed that I would perhaps be absent from school for two weeks. In reality, I seem to remember that I was absent from school for about six weeks! I developed ulcers in my mouth and found that I was unable to eat all the meals presented before me. At the age of fifteen, I was not treated to jelly and ice cream but was made to eat solid foods. It just didn't happen, and at visiting times, my mum used to hide the evidence when I didn't eat. I lost so much weight that I fainted one day, and my dad insisted that Mum was 'too soft', and he actually made me eat from that day! It didn't help, by the time I returned to school, as I had fallen behind with my work; as a perfectionist and a 'slow coach', I would struggle to catch up.

I didn't identify then, however, that the maths teacher also played a major part in my struggling as I remember each lesson when I arrived in class I would hear 'Take out your books and carry on where you left off. If you want help, ask'. That would be a typical maths lesson in Set One, and at the end, I would hear my teacher say 'See you in the next lesson and please leave quietly.'

I never did manage to cover the entire syllabus for the maths exam. In my opinion, the method of learning and lack of checking by the teacher, to confirm my learning, had failed me. I only managed to scrape through with a CSE exam in maths, and then, if my memory serves me right, it was the lowest grade achievable I think—grade five although it could have been a four.

After leaving school in 1978, I went to my local FE college to study on a secretarial course. Although I was offered a two-year diploma course, I opted for the one-year because I would be on the same course as my best friend from school. I studied a range of business subjects, including typing, shorthand, and office practice, as well as continuing with German as I had studied this at school.

I worked on Friday nights and Saturdays at a local supermarket. In those days you had to work out how much change to give the customer so my maths really wasn't so bad as I always managed to give the correct change. In addition to this, during the college holidays, I signed up with a local temping agency and knocked on the door of a local firm of solicitors. I now know I was a workaholic even back then and had the opportunity to put into practice some of the skills I had been developing. I remember having to learn to deal with difficult customers, and on one occasion, whilst at work in the supermarket, I even had a bag of potatoes thrown at me by a customer who had been caught shoplifting. On another occasion, I had an accident when collecting trolleys as I pushed them a little too forcefully through the door, so much so that the glass shattered in the door and we had to wait for a local glass company to come and repair it before being able to close up that evening.

Whilst I was working on a temping contract for a flooring company, during one of the college holidays, one of the administrators handed in her notice, and so I was offered the job and it was agreed that they would hold it open until I finished my college course. In the meantime, I was also told about another vacancy with a local building society, and I knew that this would be more suitable for me because I would rely on public transport and this route had a better service. It would also be more interesting in my opinion as I am very much a 'people person' and it would involve customer service. I discovered that my best friend had also applied for this job, and I still remember the day when she rang me to tell me she had been unsuccessful. I found it difficult therefore when I had to explain that I had been successful and had been offered the job. At first, she thought I was joking, and then when she did finally realise that I wasn't joking, I did wonder if she would ever speak to me again.

It was a difficult decision to make when I accepted the job, but I knew I had to put myself first. It didn't work out too bad as I rang to apologise to the other company who had been holding the job open for me, and I talked them into giving my best friend an interview. She forgave me and took that job.

My first full-time job was a big learning curve; I was employed as a shorthand typist/relief cashier and on the first day was told by the manager that under no circumstances should I hand over any money if any bank robbers came in demanding it. My colleagues soon put me right. They said, 'The money is insured. Our life is more important. If they want money, hand it over.' Working in the building society was interesting. On a daily basis, I had to go next door to a supermarket to buy teacakes. I then had to toast and butter them as well as boil the milk for milky coffees for my colleagues. They then had their break, which involved reading the daily newspapers, whilst I was engaged in serving the customers who came in to make their transactions. In those days, we had to calculate the interest daily, and on an odd occasion, when the cash till didn't balance, I had to balance it before I could go home.

After a few months, my best friend contacted me to tell me that there was a vacancy at the solicitors firm which she was now working for and ask me if I was interested. This was confirmation that she was still speaking to me. I attended an interview, and when asked if they could contact my current employer if I was successful, I agreed to this. The next day at work, before I had even had the time to take my coat off, the manager asked to see me and told me that the solicitors had telephoned him for a reference. Whoops! Actually, he was very nice and said he would be sorry to lose me. I hadn't even accepted the job and was a little annoyed that they had contacted him at this stage although, on reflection, they only did what they said as they were going to offer me the job. I was given a really good 'send-off', and from then on, I worked alongside my best friend for about the next three years or so. I worked in several departments, including litigation and debt collection. I still think, to this day, that this was a very valuable opportunity to learn many life skills and gain excellent experience, and since then, I have managed to resolve successfully any difficult situations such as when I wanted some faulty windows replacing and the letter I sent seemed to do the trick. I am so thankful for my days working at the solicitors firm and the words 'without prejudice' as I find it usually makes the recipients of my letters take note.

I was contacted by the temping agency I had worked for in the holidays, during my time at college. They informed me of a job which was coming available. I decided it was time to move on, and having been employed to do audio typing for the last three or so years, I realised I would have to practise my shorthand to have a chance at securing the job. It was at a brewery, and so my dad was quite excited at the prospect of free beer. I had been annoyed that my best friend had not only received a bigger pay increase than everyone else because her boss had been made a partner and she had insisted she was therefore worth more, but she had also told me about it and said not to tell anyone else. Talk about being annoyed!

I left the solicitors and took up my new position with the brewery as secretary to five area managers, two for tenanted and three for managed houses. I told my dad that he could look forward to four cases of beer every month — he couldn't believe his luck.

Working at the brewery gave me an opportunity to develop further skills and knowledge, including life experience which I think played an important part later on when I would move into teaching.

I developed good working relationships throughout my time at the brewery, which lasted just over seven years. During that time, I continued to work with the courts, when applying for licences for the pub managers and tenants. I dealt with complaints that came in because someone hadn't been happy with how they had been treated by the manager of a pub the previous night. A customer called in to complain that his trousers had been ripped on a nail that was sticking out of a seat at his local pub and that he wanted to claim on our insurance. I agreed we would be able to do this but would need his trousers as proof, before being able to deal with the claim. He didn't seem too happy at that; perhaps he thought he would keep his old pair of trousers as well as obtain a new pair. I was a quick learner. I even had to call the fire brigade when the alarm sounded one day. The director came over insisting it was a false alarm, but by that time the fire crew were outside, it was too late to cancel the call.

One day, I arrived at work to find out that we would be upgrading the typewriters to word processors, and so a colleague and I decided we would enrol on a local college course to learn the techniques of this new technology. It was whilst I was at college that I noticed a course available for anyone wanting to teach Office Studies.

From an early age, I had wanted to teach. I remember very vividly that my father, who was a joiner by trade, had made me a matching desk, chair, and chalk board and that I used to line up my teddy bears and dolls to have their maths lesson — you see I did like maths at one time, before those awful lessons!

Illustrated by Joel John Lambert

Anyway, I decided to enrol on the Royal Society of Arts Teacher Training course in Office Studies. I chose typewriting as my first subject and embarked on a four-term course when I learned a great deal from a teacher who would later become my mentor. I had nothing but respect for her. She had traits very similar to my own; as a perfectionist, she only accepted the highest quality in everything and so always challenged me to strive for my best every time.

Chapter 2

My Early Teaching Years

Having qualified to teach typewriting, I decided that I wanted to continue with my job at the brewery, which I enjoyed so much, and teach this subject as an evening class at my local FE college, where I had trained myself after leaving school and had already taught some classes. I signed up with the local council to indicate my interest in working for them when someone pointed out to me that there was a job advertised for a teacher on a part-time basis at another college not far from where I lived. I decided to investigate further and so applied for the job. I wondered if there would be an opportunity to teach some sessions in the evenings.

I was invited to interview, and, as I waited in reception, I could guess who the other candidates were. During the interview, I learned that the job would be two days a week and that the pay was equivalent to what I was earning in my present full-time job. I had fallen in love with this place. It inspired me, but there were no opportunities to teach evening classes, so I had a dilemma: Should I retain the security of my full-time position that I knew to be safe or should I take a risk and opt for the two days. I didn't really think I would be offered the job anyway.

I was asked to deliver two short sessions to demonstrate my teaching skills, and the first was a fifteen-minute session in Office Practice studies. I can't remember exactly what I had to do, but I distinctly remember a mature adult student asking if I was free that evening for a date. This was to be a sign of things to come – dealing with such issues when I had little experience. I came up with some funny answer which gave everyone a laugh, and I managed to steer away from the embarrassment.

I remember more clearly the second session I was tasked to deliver which was to work with six students and get them to practise the 'home keys' on the typewriter. I remember, as though it was only yesterday, asking them to place their fingers on the 'home keys' and then starting to drill them by calling out ASDF ;LKJ. It was only then I realised that they had all started to practise the drills without any paper in the typewriters. Their instructor had asked them to do exactly what I asked them, and as I hadn't asked them to insert paper into the typewriters, they hadn't! After the initial hiccup, I asked them to put paper in the typewriters, and everything went well after that. I had survived!

Following these sessions, I had the formal interview, when I was asked whether I was too young and inexperienced to do a job like this. I remember thinking, 'Well, I am twenty-seven.' Imagine if someone asked that these days with equality. After being invited to have lunch and a tour, one candidate apologised that she couldn't stay, and those of us remaining accepted. I thought that the lady who had left had a far better chance of securing the job as she had lots more experience than me.

After a great deal of thought and even though I didn't expect to be successful, I decided I had to contact the college and explain that I wouldn't want to lose the security of my full-time job and that if anything came up in the future, I would most certainly be interested. I was in a state of shock when I was asked, 'Is that the only reason?' My heart started to race, and my colleague working in the office at that time stopped what she was doing when she saw the look on my face. I sensed something was about to happen.

About an hour later, I received a call asking if I would take the job on a full-time basis. I can remember the absolute excitement in my voice as I immediately replied, 'Yes'.

Then I had to break the news to my colleague, my boss, and even more so my family. My mum was worried and asked if I knew what I was doing: leaving a job I loved to take such a risk with the unknown. Over twenty years later, I have never looked back! She now knows I took a calculated risk for the better.

I started my full-time teaching career in 1989, working in the Business Studies Department, and I was responsible for teaching students Office Practice and word-processing.

Working with adults ranging in age from sixteen to sixty-five (anyone basically of employment age), I covered such topics in Office Practice as how to write a cheque as younger students had not experienced this and it would help them to ensure that when carrying out this task for themselves, they did not do anything to endanger their monies by forgetting to put the name of the payee in, for example. Even back then, I would make it as realistic as possible to engage the students. I took in my own cheque book and wrote out cheques as necessary, before issuing some blank cheques that I had made myself for the students to practise with.

I remember a quiz I had created during my teacher training to assess learning in respect of Office Practice, and one of the questions was to list ten items you could find in an office. One student really tested my patience by answering the question as follows:

List ten items you could find in an office.

1   Yucca plant
2   Yucca plant
3   Yucca plant
4   Yucca plant
5   Yucca plant
6   Yucca plant

7 Yucca plant
8 Yucca plant
9 Yucca plant
10 Yucca plant

As I asked the student to join me in the corridor, so I could speak in private, I wondered how I would deal with the matter if I didn't get a favourable response. Luckily, he did as he was asked, and I spent five minutes explaining to him that I would not tolerate his behaviour and that he should take the lessons seriously if he wanted to get anywhere in life. The next day, I had a surprise left for me on my desk—it was a yucca plant!

The word-processing sessions only allowed for three students at any one time because that was the number of dedicated machines the college had with 8-inch floppy disks too. I was continuing with my teacher training and was now aiming to achieve a teaching certificate in word-processing and using a different system to the versions at the different establishments where I was teaching. This certainly made for fun during sessions when I would give the wrong commands to carry out a function. I soon learnt to admit I wasn't perfect and would get mixed up between control and c and alt and c, for example, to copy something. In those early days, it would all be based on commands as a mouse wasn't part of the computer set-up.

After finishing the Teacher Training Certificate in word-processing, I went on to do my final RSA Certificate in Teacher Training, which was in IT, and this required me to learn to use spreadsheets, databases, and graphics packages to enhance my existing skills. It was whilst in these afternoon sessions that I became friends with two other ladies whom I would go on to work with over the years as part of a committee for the STBE (Society for Teachers in Business Education).

I not only joined the committee but also acted as chair and was involved in organising the annual national conference. We had a really engaging programme that we had arranged, and the setting for the hotel was overlooking Nottingham Castle. This was my first experience of teaching other teachers when I delivered sessions on using PowerPoint for presentations to colleagues. I remember how nervous I was back then, but I soon relaxed during the evening dinner, following a welcome from the Lord Mayor, when we were entertained by strolling minstrels (men in green tights supposed to be Robin Hood and his merry men).

It was at this time I was asked to teach desktop publishing, and when I asked what it was, I was told to go away and find out. I promptly did so, talking to some of the students who were already engaged in this subject. The students had about six computers which were the first in the college to have hard disk drives. They had hard disk drives of 20 mb, 640k of RAM, and a mouse and used a 'run-time' version of Windows. It was then I had to get used to using menu-driven software to copy, print, and save rather than the familiar commands I had used for a few years.

Desktop publishing was used by the students to produce origination artwork for the print industry, and we had our own print workshop on campus. We produced business cards, flyers, and a range of other advertising materials, and it was then that I first met my husband. He was a student at the time, who had transferred from our FE Department into the Business Studies Department, and he came to me for sessions on a daily basis. I remember one occasion when he arrived late for his session. When I challenged his lateness, as I was always a stickler for time-keeping, he asked if I wanted the truth or not. When he said it was because of a spider, I certainly thought he had good imagination. However, I now know he was being serious, having married him some time after he had left college when our paths crossed again. One evening when the biggest spider I had seen walked across our lounge floor, Mark almost stopped breathing! I also required my learners to dress appropriately for an office, and on this same day, a member of parliament was visiting the college. Mark was wearing jeans, and I was so angry that I told him to make sure he didn't move from under the desk as the MP came into the room.

I have met quite a few famous people over the years at different establishments where I have worked. In particular, I remember meeting the Queen and Prince Philip, Prince Philip on two separate occasions. Although I am myself very small in stature, I couldn't believe when I met the Queen that she was even smaller than me. I was at an awards ceremony when the Queen was the guest of honour. After the awards ceremony had finished, the Queen and Prince Philip were taken along a line of guests who were waiting anxiously to meet them, like you see at the Royal Variety Performance. I hadn't been chosen, so I relaxed and wanted to enjoy the moment. One of the award winners and her mother were introduced to the Queen, and suddenly, as she was nervous, her mother said that I was the teacher and pushed me in front to meet the Queen. I was thrown by this and didn't even curtsey. The Queen started talking to me, and I haven't got a clue what she said and what I had replied with. I just remember being amazed at her beauty with a face just like that of a china doll.

I was given the opportunity to sign up with a local university to work towards my Certificate in Education on a day release course. Although

I had achieved my teaching qualifications in several Office Studies subjects, as it wasn't the City & Guilds teaching qualification, I was told I would not be able to receive accreditation for prior learning and it would be therefore necessary to complete two years. I challenged this, and a lady who was head of in-service teacher training paid a visit to me at college. She was amazed when she saw the evidence I was able to present — schemes of work, lesson plans, and a wealth of resources as much of the work carried out was for customers of our print workshop. After that, it was agreed that I could receive accreditation for the first six months of the course, which I was very pleased about.

It is this same lady, Val, who would later inspire me to write this book. Our paths crossed again, some twenty years after my training on the CertEd, when we met at a local meeting of the Morgan Sports Car Club, and I told her how it had always been an ambition of mine to write a book. She suggested I should write about my experience as a subject learning coach.

When I joined the CertEd course, I met other teachers in training from local FE colleges, and I think at first they didn't realise the level of work being done at my college. It was only when we started looking at teachers becoming 'facilitators' and I was already experiencing this with students starting on a roll-on/roll-off basis that the other teachers in the group looked to me for advice and guidance on how to manage this type of learning.

In the lessons, rather than there being a lesson plan for the group, I had an overall plan for the group working on their own individual SMART goals, and as real work would very often come in at any time during the lesson, I had work prepared for the students but would change this as necessary to ensure that the real jobs were produced by students who had the relevant skills and would benefit from the work to be carried out. This worked well as it helped to build the students' confidence when they saw the finished printed work ready and waiting for the customer to collect.

I was also asked to go to the City & Guilds Examination Board in London to help develop a qualification for desktop publishing. They were pleased with my ideas, and the exam was eventually put into circulation, and the tasks were all based around the type of work undertaken in our college.

In 1992, I achieved my Certificate in Education and got married to Mark and then embarked on the next stage of my development. Incidentally, did I mention that as part of my CertEd training, I had to visit two educational establishments and so I went back to my old C of E primary school and my old comprehensive school? Who do you think I bumped into as I went to the reception desk at my old comprehensive school? You guessed right, my maths teacher, and he enquired why I was visiting. When I told him that I was training to be a teacher, I seem to remember him commenting on the fact he was surprised as I was never that clever, hence the title of my book!

At college, we worked with people having disabilities to get them back into employment. Some students may have had an accident at work or an illness which meant that they could not do a manual job any longer. When assisting them to gain new skills, we were always ahead of the game, and by keeping in touch with the needs of employers, we were forever changing the skills we would deliver to meet the needs of employers. I have worked with students with a varied range of disabilities, including people with brain and spinal injuries, cerebral palsy, autism, epilepsy, fibromyalgia, amputees, and arthritis (the latter which I have myself and can fully relate therefore to the difficulties that the students have when dealing with a disability).

One of my students, many years ago, wanted to become famous — either an actor or a member of a band. I spent hours telling him that he had to be realistic and learn about administration and he could think about acting or becoming a member of a band in his spare time as he needed to get a proper job that would bring in a regular wage. Some years later, when I went to see the pantomime *Snow White and the Seven*

Dwarfs at a local theatre, the narrator was announcing forthcoming birthdays for children in the audience. He then suddenly asked if I was in the audience and if I would stand up. My face changed to the colour of beetroot as I stood up in the middle of the auditorium, and he announced, 'Your student told you he would become famous one day.' I should mention here that apart from being in the pantomime, he had also acted in some very famous children's films.

I was constantly developing my own skills and became qualified as an assessor to deliver national vocational qualification programmes; I also achieved another qualification to become an internal verifier, and the list went on. Continual professional development was very important to me as I was passionate about learning.

I was asked to become a mentor for other staff, and this included the need to observe lessons and give feedback for development. I attended a development day at the same university where I gained my Certificate in Education in order to gain experience in this new field. My tutor, Val, was delighted to 'have me on board' as a mentor.

I had previously applied for a job to teach at my local college of further education and was unsuccessful. My teacher and mentor at the college who was the department head informed me that the reason for my not getting the job was that I would most likely regret leaving my current job.

She knew me well and backed up what she was saying by mentioning that when answering questions in the interview, I constantly referred to the college where I worked, and it was obvious that I had a passion for the place! It was at this time, when I started to mentor staff who were in teacher training, that I decided I would only leave my job, which I loved so much to teach teachers as this was my other passion — to raise the standards in teaching and learning and make learning a most enjoyable time for learners. I didn't want anyone to experience what I had gone through all those years ago in my maths lessons. I realised that instead of making learning fun just for my students, I could also make the same impact on other students by sharing my good practices with their teachers. This way, I could spread the fun across more and more students.

I was also aware that in general, teachers and colleges did not want to share ideas and resources and try to always be better than the others in the competition. In my opinion, it was such a shame to keep some really good practice in isolation. I identified the benefits of sharing ideas and resources when carrying out observations of staff as I truly came away each time with ideas to put into practice. Since that day, I have seen so many examples of excellent work in sessions and have embraced them always, by incorporating the ideas in my own sessions and sharing ideas with the staff I was mentoring.

At this time, our department was very strong. We had a training manager, who had the vision to identify what the employers wanted, and a senior tutor, whose high standards assisted the college to achieve Investors in People for the first time. Quality improvements were important to us as a team, and in particular, we would carry out observations on each other (peer observations) and internally verify our work as assessors. We would also be observed by external verifiers to check we were doing everything as we should be. I now know that peer observations are most valuable to develop and improve sessions, and I agree with what Joyce and Showers suggest and certainly recommend that you look up peer observations. To read their findings, refer to the research carried out by Joyce and Showers (Joyce, B, and Showers, B (1996), The Evolution of Peer Coaching, Educational Leadership, 53 (6): 12-16.

With the Internet becoming more popular in the year 2000, the college was given some funding by the Ian Karten Charitable Trust to develop a CTEC Centre (computer-aided training, education, and communication) – three rooms, including powerful new equipment, furniture, and industrial software (Macromedia products) to deliver training in web page design.

Ian was a very clever man, who was once introduced to a young man who was disabled and needed to use a communication aid to communicate. From that point onwards, Ian decided that he would set up a trust fund to assist people with disabilities to communicate using ICT. For further information about Ian Karten's story, see the website www.karten-network.org.uk.

I was part of a small team, and we were given the opportunity to attend some specialist training in Leamington Spa. To say that we were all teachers and so responsible adults, we all missed our stop on the train and so had to get off at the next station and beg the station master to let us go back to Leamington Spa. We developed our skills together and then agreed who would take responsibility for each of the three packages, Dreamweaver to produce web sites, Flash for animation, and Fireworks for designing graphics.

In my opinion working with others in an action learning set was very powerful to aid our learning, rather than working in isolation. We developed resources and tried them out on each other before using them for training the students. We were enthusiastic and highly motivated to succeed, and by bringing in 'real work' from customers to design and produce websites, this was a fantastic learning approach to use with the students. They were all engaged fully in the work they were set and were able to appreciate softer skills such as working in a team, meeting deadlines and customer service.

After several successful placements for our students, and as web design vacancies required more programming and graphic design skills, we had to consider new courses, and we decided to go down the route of Microsoft Office packages and Sage for accounts. At about this time (2002), the college structure was also undergoing a change, and I was promoted to team leader for Business Administration and Customer Service.

I was asked to attend some training in Kent for a week, all expenses paid by the college, and it would be intensive to develop Microsoft Office programs. As I had been teaching web page design, my Microsoft Office skills were a little rusty. I was reassured that there was nothing to worry about but to just go and make the most of the opportunity.

I booked into a nice hotel with a spa so I could make the most of my time in the evening, going for a swim as I would be on my own. I soon received a shock when I discovered that I would be expected to take online exams to become a Microsoft Office master instructor in order that our college could become a testing centre for Microsoft Office exams. I only managed to grab a breakfast on the first morning and certainly didn't get anywhere near the swimming pool because I spent my evenings practising for the exams.

By the Friday, I had achieved all the exams required except one. I achieved exams in PowerPoint, Outlook, Access, and the required advanced level in Word. I managed to also achieve Excel, but I needed to achieve this program at advanced level, and my time had run out.

I got back to work the following week and had a word with my colleague who had omitted to mention the exams. I then contacted the trainer from the previous week to find out when I could take the final exam necessary. She booked me in for a two-day course, which would be in Manchester. I travelled by train after work and booked into the hotel which had been recommended. I was looking forward to seeing Emma, who had been the trainer in Kent. I decided to have a walk out and make sure I knew where I needed to go for the training on the following day. The venue for the training was on Portland Street, and I found it quite easily. I called in a restaurant to grab a bite to eat before retiring to my room with a book on Excel. I was dreading this one as lacking in confidence with my maths skills, I wondered how I would get on with the spreadsheet program.

The next morning, I was up and had breakfast, and then off I went to Portland Street for my training day. As I walked along Portland Street, I suddenly realised that the number I was looking for just wasn't there. I had the letterhead from the company who I would be training with but could not find it however hard I looked.

Eventually, I stopped a taxi driver to ask for help, and he suggested I jump in the taxi as it was a different Portland Street on an industrial estate just outside the city. He dropped me off at the door to the company and left. I went to reception to ask where I needed to be for the training, and they informed me that in actual fact, this was their head office, but the training was taking place at another place, which was back in the city on the road adjacent to Portland Street. They called me a taxi, and off I went back to where I had come from.

By this time, I was late arriving and the training had already started. As if that wasn't enough, I was also put on a network computer called New York, and it was 11 September, the anniversary of the Twin Towers attack. The computer just would not work, and so I had to move to another one. Just before lunch, the fire alarm sounded, and as we all looked at each other, I suggested that we should evacuate the building. At that moment, there was a big bang, and we all thought that a bomb had gone off. The fire alarm then sounded again.

We found out that we should have been informed but did not receive the message that the fire alarm was sounded, followed by a two-minute silence, gun fire from the market place, and then the end of the two-minute silence marked with another fire alarm sounding.

Could anything else go wrong? I achieved the exam I needed and arranged with the trainer to go for a meal at the end of the day. By early evening, I was very tired and went to my hotel room to get a good night's sleep. At around 2 am, I was disturbed by the phone ringing. I answered it only to find that there was a rather drunk-sounding male asking me if he could come to my room. I was certain that he had just phoned as a prank and that he didn't really know which my room was. Even so I couldn't go back to sleep as I was listening at the door just in case.

The next morning, I gathered together my suitcase, laptop, and bag and was just about to get in the lift to go and check out when the fire alarm started. I had heavy bags and had to walk down five flights of stairs, which did not go down too well. What a time I had in Manchester — it almost doesn't seem possible that such things could happen!

Chapter 3

My First Real Experience of Ofsted

My first real experience with Ofsted was in November 2004. Although I had known several inspections before, it was the first time that I was directly involved. As team leader for Business Administration and Customer Service, I went to meet my Ofsted inspector in reception. We recognised each other straight away as we were the ones wearing suits! Obviously, we both had a professional background in business, and so rather than being more casually dressed, we were the odd ones out.

I felt well prepared for this moment as I had read through detailed information about what to expect, including what judgements would be based on. I did this in style too as I read the information during a visit to the Champagne Bar in St Pancras train station after attending a board meeting in London.

I also recall that I had been introduced to Gervase Phinn, who was an after-dinner speaker at a function I attended. Gervase Phinn was an Ofsted inspector, who had written books about some of his memories and experiences when carrying out school inspections. I bought some of his books and laughed so much when reading them that I was very relaxed about the Ofsted visit.

The other areas of the college being inspected included Information and Communication Technology, Independent Living Skills, Literacy, Numeracy and Communication, and Pre-Vocational Studies. I was the only representative in my area whilst the other areas had at least two representatives, who were able to support each other through the inspection process. I was excited to have the experience although it was fair to say that I was a little nervous.

My inspector put me at ease immediately, and I found the whole experience both enjoyable and very rewarding. Others thought I was 'mad', but my inspector and I had a mutual respect, and my honesty and integrity were evident. I learnt a great deal from the experience. We would meet every morning and afternoon to discuss findings, and he would ask questions, and if he needed evidence, I would be given an opportunity to collect it for the next scheduled meeting.

At that time, I had a tutor group which I managed on a full-time basis as well as had my team leader duties. I was younger in those days, but it was still exhausting. I was observed when delivering a text processing session. I remember we were working on producing memos, and I related this to my husband's organisation as although email was now very popular and used in offices, in some organisations, eg, on the factory shop floor, the employees would not have access to email.

The session went well even though I seem to remember I only had three students and one of them had to leave early for a medical appointment. I reflected and felt that whilst this didn't give me a full opportunity to shine, it did evidence that I am flexible and able to adapt sessions to meet the needs of individual students. I ensured that the student having to leave early knew he could come back and see me the following day for further activities, and I emailed other students who were not in the session to invite them to make an appointment with me to go through the activities. Where possible, I challenged the students who had attended the session to demonstrate their learning to the other students as I feel it is important to use peers to support each other. This develops their self-confidence and consolidates their own learning.

In another session, I had a mature student who had difficulty with his speech, following a stroke, and he was conscious of this so as another student was going on holiday to Spain, I suggested he might help her by joining in some Spanish lessons. My strategy worked well, and gradually, he regained his confidence whilst learning some Spanish. They were both able to order food and drinks as well as ask for the bill!

I always try to generate 'real work' activities as in my opinion this is far more valuable than just working towards exams. I was proved correct when one of my students successfully achieved Microsoft Office Master status having taken online exams in Access, PowerPoint, Outlook, Word, and Excel (the latter two at advanced level). However, when I gave him a complex table and report to do in Word, he needed considerable support to achieve the end result. This suggests that he had trained specifically to meet the requirements of the exams but couldn't put the skills into practice to produce the work given.

Another two of my students were acting as stock clerks for the department and were working in the stockroom, undertaking a stock check. My Ofsted inspector would appear from nowhere and ask them question after question to check their learning. I was then, without realising, putting the emphasis on their learning rather than my teaching.

I have used a cartoon below to demonstrate that it should all be about the learning and not the teaching. One girl said to the other that she had taught her hamster to sing. The other girl replied that she couldn't hear the hamster singing. The first girl said, 'I taught my hamster to sing, but I didn't say she learnt it!'

Illustrated by Joel John Lambert

I really like this as I believe it expressed very well that it should always be about the learning and not the teacher 'teaching' from the front of the classroom. I will talk about this further in a later chapter.

The Ofsted visit went very well for me and the other team members, and this was reflected in the Ofsted report in which it inferred that our 'model' should be cascaded across the college. Teaching and learning had been graded as satisfactory (grade 3) with the exception of our team, and we received a good (grade 2).

I was so proud when I read the report as I was praised by my Ofsted inspector for my outstanding leadership and management. It made me feel extremely valued and gave me an awareness of my skills and attributes which I hadn't previously even thought about except perhaps when my husband came to pick me up and needed to use the loo, to my surprise, he told me that mine was the only name not mentioned on the toilet walls! On reflection, the inspection process was a very valuable learning experience for me. I learnt so much, and I was highly motivated and inspired by my Ofsted inspector. I wasn't aware, at that time however, that our paths would cross again and would lead to a whole new chapter of my life beginning.

My Sincere Thanks to Gervase Phinn for Keeping Me Going Before and During Our Ofsted Inspection

My thanks to Gervase
For writing his books
When laughing out loud
I got some funny looks

Sitting in the champagne bar
At St Pancras train station
A glass of pink champagne
I didn't need much persuasion

Preparing for an Ofsted
He inspired me so much
I had to keep on reading
He had a magic touch

He kept me sane
When the inspectors arrived
No way would I miss it
And I survived

Thank you once more
For getting me through it
What a fabulous experience
And there was nothing to it

Now I look forward
To Ofsted arriving
Others think I am mad
And it is all about surviving

Chapter 4

New Learning Experiences

One day in January 2005, when the telephone rang, one of my students answered it as this was another chance for them to build their self-confidence. I was informed that it was my Ofsted inspector wanting to speak to me. I was shocked and started to wonder if I had done something wrong. He asked me if I had received any information from the Standards Unit. I replied that I hadn't. How embarrassing it was when he mentioned that he thought he had seen a box in my room during the inspection! Sure enough I scanned the room, and there was the box! He explained to me that the Standards Unit had been tasked by the Department for Education to raise the standards in teaching and learning, and he invited me to attend a one-day conference for teachers and trainers in business administration.

I agreed to go along to find out more about it, and this was my introduction to the Subject Learning Coach programme. This was possibly the most valuable opportunity that I have ever had, and I owe it all to my Ofsted inspector!

I attended my first of many network meetings, where I had the opportunity to meet other teachers and trainers with whom I could network and share ideas and resources relating to business administration. The day began with an icebreaker (after refreshments of course). We all had to mingle and ask questions if my memory serves me well. This was a fun way to introduce ourselves and something

I would take back and use in my sessions when new students started. Then the aims of the day were shared with delegates, and we then set about sharing good practices through lots of 'hands-on' activities known as 'active learning'. As the day went on, I was not only enjoying myself and engaging fully but also found it both a pleasure and rewarding to be working with like-minded people.

I was being introduced to action learning sets and active learning, and I found these to be very powerful and effective strategies to use in education. I could compare this experience to what was a factor for our success in achieving the grade 2 in the Ofsted inspection—the fact that we worked together as a team (action learning set) meant that our resources and planning were innovative through inspiring one another.

I think the reason for this was that I was sharing ideas with peers relating to the subjects I taught. Previously, as a team leader, I was chosen to work with other team leaders. This was another example of action learning sets. However, this was less effective in my opinion as the team leaders were from different departments in the college such as physiotherapy, fundraising, and teaching and learning. We all had different goals and priorities and therefore found it difficult to agree on what we wanted to achieve as an action learning set.

By the end of the networking day, my interest had been captured, thanks to the passion and energy demonstrated by the facilitators. I had been witness to so many examples of best practices, and I wanted to go back to college and share them all with work colleagues, especially my team. It was going to prove difficult as I still had a full-time teaching commitment and the additional duties in my role as team leader. However, I was able to identify some time on a travel day (these are days when residential students travel home for the holidays and return after the holidays).

I arranged to facilitate a session to 'show and tell' my team and others some of the ideas I had seen demonstrated at the Standards Unit event. I planned my session based on this event and suggested that the colleagues use active learning in their sessions, and I explained the importance of it. I also explained the action learning set techniques and value of using them. We discussed the benefits of icebreakers and/or starter activities which could be either an activity to recap the previous session's topic or an activity to introduce the theme of the session. I also suggested that the word 'quiz' be used rather than 'test' when assessing learning! I remember supporting two colleagues to learn how to use Microsoft Office Word, and one of them obviously had bad memories of his school days as every time I welcomed them to the session and mentioned that I wanted them to work through the quick quiz I had prepared, this colleague would always comment that it was going to be another test!

I was really pleased when my Ofsted inspector confirmed he would be able to come into college and do a 'show and tell' session using activities from the Standard Unit's box that had been left in my classroom. As my preferred learning style is to be shown and then 'have a go' (I remember the impact of those maths sessions – my good experience and later bad experience), this suited my learning style perfectly, and the rest of my team joined us, which was fantastic as they all had a great respect for our Ofsted inspector.

I signed up for the next network meeting, which included a 'show and tell' session, and I agreed to use an activity to engage the other teachers based on the television programme 'Blockbusters', which one of my colleagues had shared with me. This went really well as rather than just explaining how it worked, I actually got the delegates into teams and used a general knowledge quiz to demonstrate how it worked. I used a projector to show the Word document I had created, along with different coloured hexagons which I used to cover the letters as a team got an answer correct. As we didn't have buzzers, I distributed some items for this purpose, i.e., bells and a 'wiggle stick', which I had bought from a children's store. I also had a squeaky toy, which I borrowed from a dog!

The winning team were presented with a box of Quality Street, which I encouraged them to share with the rest of the group. Again, I had been inspired by ideas I had seen demonstrated and once more had lots of ideas to take back and use. The whole event had been planned in detail, using active learning to engage us and modelling good practice.

The starter activity had been a great idea as when delegates arrived for the event, they had something to do if they didn't know anybody or feel confident enough to chat (something I have never had a problem with)! One strategy that I liked in particular was that we were given some post-it notes to use if we wanted to ask a question but didn't have the confidence to ask in front of a large group of delegates. We were asked to stick them on the wall, and they would be looked at during the break time, and answers given before we started the next activity.

I compared the experience of these events to my experience when undertaking the CertEd, and on reflection, whilst some of the lecturers inspired me, I will always remember the lecture about methods of learning and how to teach using a range of teaching methods. The whole lecture consisted of someone at the front of the lecture room 'telling' us what techniques we should use. I think it was a real shame that they didn't model good practice whilst delivering the session but only shared theories with us.

Although I had been in the teaching profession since 1989, it was only when I started to work in a team and use action research and active learning to share resources and bounce ideas off other members of my team and trial activities we came up with that we started to vastly improve the learning experience for our students.

Chapter 5

Inspired

By having the opportunity to be part of the business administration network meetings with the Standards Unit, I was inspired to develop new innovative resources and have the confidence to take risks. Sometimes, a new approach I tried did not work well, but instead of giving up, I kept making changes and revisiting the approach again and again until eventually after three or four attempts, I would get it right, for the benefit of the students.

Another thing I discovered early on was not to always say you know something when you don't. Other tutors I had observed were afraid that they would not be credible if they admitted that they did not know something. Instead, what I would always say is that I might not know everything but the main thing is to know where to find the answers to questions. In fact, I would encourage learners to find out answers themselves to their questions as this would make them 'independent learners'. In this respect, I believe, as had been suggested, that learners who have been 'spoon-fed' (also known as 'shallow learning') would later drop out of university because they didn't know how to learn independently.

In addition to the network meetings, I was asked if I would like to undertake the Subject Learning Coach Professional Training Programme (SLC PTP). I can't recall whether this was still under the Standards Unit as it later changed to the Quality Improvement Agency

(QIA). I joined a cohort, and this professional programme included several residential events. It was so wonderful to be working again with like-minded people, who all had a passion for making the learning experience one of fun and engagement. This was a most powerful journey, and I soaked up so much knowledge and experience just like a sponge absorbs liquid!

I was introduced to many excellent models and protocols, ten pedagogical approaches and coaching techniques. I think that pedagogy is a word that has come here from America and simply means 'the science of teaching'. I remember a lady I met at a dinner party who lectured in a university and had been asked to go to Italy to speak to lecturers over there and share her methods of teaching. She had been asked to include something about pedagogy and asked me what it was as she had never heard of it before.

I have referred to some of the models, protocols, and pedagogies in this book and would recommend you go to the Excellence Gateway website, www.excellencegateway.org.uk, where you will find some brilliant cards to explain more about them. The details of where to find them is given in the 'Further Reading' section at the end of this book. I was very proud to achieve accreditation from Oxford Brookes University in conjunction with the Centre of Excellence for Learning (CEL). Previously, I had been involved in action learning sets when a management consultancy organisation came to work with team leaders as mentioned in an earlier chapter. However, it was during the SLC PTP that I fully understood the concept of action learning sets.

When using action learning sets on the SLC PTP, we worked in triads to practise our coaching skills and came to conclusions and found answers to our own questions and needs. Each triad would include a person doing the coaching, one being coached, and another observing the coaching session and giving feedback. I believe that the coaching techniques we used were possibly the most powerful new tool I learned and began to realise that although you might go to your colleague or line manager for answers, the best answers by far are arrived at when you find your own solutions, and this is done through asking the right questions. The model I use to coach myself and others is the GROW model, as devised by Sir John Whitmore (see 'Further Reading' section for more information).

I can thoroughly recommend that you consider referring to the GROW model to help you to find solutions to problems and issues as well as use it as a tool to improve your sessions, in order to enable the learners to have fun!

An example of my using the GROW model was when I was asked to move on a full-time basis into a classroom which I knew would be unsuitable as a lot of the work I was involved in was very confidential. I used the GROW to help me reflect on this before rushing in, and in fact, this worked well as I was able to keep a desk in another room so that when I needed to, I could do the confidential work necessary. It also helped my colleagues as in the testing centre, where my desk was then based, I was also able to oversee the exams for their students whilst they carried on working with their other students.

Again, through the SLC PTP, I learned about emotional intelligence (look for Daniel Goleman to learn more about this). It is suggested that whilst a certain amount of intelligence is needed to do a job, it is of great value if a person also has emotional intelligence. In fact, research suggests that the most successful managers or coaches are those with emotional intelligence. I undertook an emotional intelligence inventory, which helped me identify that I have a very high level of emotional intelligence, and I also identified the areas that I should develop, one of them being not to rush in when faced with something I disliked, eg, change but to reflect and use the GROW model to identify how I would deal with a situation.

As you will probably realise, from what you have read so far, I saw the opportunity to take part in the Subject Learning Coach programme to be a most wonderful chance to develop my existing skills and to learn new techniques and protocols to complement them. I was inspired and continually soaked up more and more knowledge through the programme and network meetings.

As I developed in the programme, my confidence increased to take more and more risks and try new things out in my sessions. I had realised very quickly that it was no longer about the teacher teaching students but it was about students learning from a range of active learning tasks that I could then use to assess that learning was taking place. Remember the two girls and the singing hamster?

When we talk about active learning and assessment of learning then, examples of these could be using a quiz which could be in the format of a jigsaw, Blockbusters, bingo, or card activities. They are all active because the students engage in the activity, the activities are fun, and learning can be assessed by observing what students are able to answer. Even if a student gets an answer wrong, by asking other students until the right answer is given will then reinforce the correct answer even for the student who got it wrong to begin with, and the students are therefore helping each other to learn.

The SLC PTP was very challenging, and I remember that each time I had attended a 'residential', which was about one a month, I was required to produce an assignment. Now to add to my hectic work days, I also had hectic weekends as most of them were spent in my office, and at home I worked on the assignments. It was very hard and tiring, but I knew that I needed to ensure the assignment was completed before going on another 'residential' in order to give me a good chance of completing the work required on time. Some others on the programme still hadn't written their first assignment when we were coming towards the end of the programme. I feel that being organised is one of my good qualities — being able to plan and organise myself effectively, as required to be a good teacher. Remember that planning and preparation prevents poor performance! I think I truly deserved the recognition from Oxford Brookes University and almost ended up being exhausted by it all.

Chapter 6

Advancing My Coaching Skills

At one of the network meetings I attended, I discovered that there was an opportunity to advance my coaching skills by signing up for another programme on offer – to become an advanced learning coach.

Because of my experiences and inspiration through the SLC PTP, I asked to be considered for a place on the Advance Learning Coach training programme and again had to 'sweet talk' my husband into allowing me to pack a suitcase and leave him to fend for himself. I made sure that his favourite microwave meals were in the freezer before I left for the hotel where I knew I would have nice meals and wine in the evenings! However, I must say, so as not to give the wrong impression, that I did work very hard during the day and evening with lots of reading and preparation for the following day that was necessary.

By the end of the two days on the residential programme to become an advanced learning coach, I had learnt even more models and theories – in particular I remember being inspired by the facilitator, Geoff, who had a passion for Boyatzis and my sense of humour. Boyatzis's Model of Intentional Change uses a formula for an individual to move from a New Year's resolution approach to a long-lasting change in behaviour. When this model and others were introduced, rather than just being given the theory, we were given an activity to do which demonstrated the model.

During the programme, we were given time to work in triads to practise our coaching skills further, and something struck me about this in that whenever we had practised our coaching skills, when attending network meetings, and when undertaking the SLC PTP, we were not observed by the facilitators, which I think was so that we would not feel uncomfortable. Then it happened—we were asked if any of us would be prepared to coach a colleague for everyone in the room to observe. I realised that this was an opportunity for me to get some feedback from all the facilitators and the other participants, and so I offered! I actually found it to be so helpful because I received feedback which indicated that I did really well with my coaching skills, and I was able to ask for further guidance where I felt I should have done more.

As per usual, I went away with more work to do, and this would include my developing the plan I had outlined to deliver the Subject Learning Coach Professional Training Programme back in my college. It was a week before the summer holidays (unlike some other colleges, I only get the last two weeks in August), and I had planned to work on the programme I wanted to deliver. I had decided that it would run over five days in total and would incorporate time for the participants to use the website for the SLC programme and produce resources to use in sessions.

Then, my world turned upside down as a result of my husband being rushed into hospital one Sunday afternoon. Mark had experienced migraines before, but this one was different, and when I realised just how much pain he was in, I asked if he wanted me to call an ambulance. He did so I knew that it was serious because throughout his life he has had to deal with his disability and has been confined to a wheelchair since about the age of twelve. I knew only too well how he copes with so many challenges and pain on a daily basis.

I called 999, which was scary, but then, as a first-aider, my training kicked in, and I kept the necessary checks on Mark whilst changing into something suitable as I had been out in the garden sunbathing when all this had occurred. I went into the conservatory to shut all the windows and locked up and gathered my things together. The paramedic was the first to arrive and having checked Mark's blood pressure asked if he usually had very high blood pressure. I am certain that this made his blood pressure rise even higher! The paramedic confirmed that an ambulance was required, and when it arrived, we put Mark into the ambulance, and I was going with him. We were told we couldn't bring his wheelchair, and so I agreed I would return home for it later.

The moment I saw the ambulance, it triggered my PTSD (post-traumatic stress disorder) that I had been suffering from, following a tragic road traffic collision locally when I had gone to help being a first-aider. I hadn't been able to save the young child, and now seeing the ambulance, especially with the paramedic's car parked in front, brought back memories of that fatal evening.

I thought on three separate occasions that I was going to lose my husband: the first being when we arrived at the Accident and Emergency Department of the hospital and Mark and I were placed in the corridor to wait until someone could assess his condition. I had read so many stories in the newspapers and seen reports on the news about people being left in hospital corridors and dying before being attended to that I suddenly found myself in a panic.

Mark was eventually assessed and given morphine intravenously for the pain. He was moved into another room, where we were told to wait until someone came to collect him to take him for a CT scan. When he was collected, I was put into the relatives' room and again thought about all those hospital programmes on the television, where relatives had been given bad news. This was my second time of thinking I was losing him, and it seemed to take forever before anyone came to see me. I had been told I could use the telephone in the room if I wanted to contact anyone, and as I didn't want to worry my family and Mark had already insisted not to say anything to his, I rang my very good friend, Jenny, only to get through to a recorded message.

Eventually, as the nurse entered the room, I held my breath, and she quickly reassured me that Mark was back in the next room and I could go and sit with him. By this time, his conversation wasn't making any sense, and I think this was a side effect of the morphine. He was moved to a 'critical' ward, next down from intensive care, and once he had been made as comfortable as possible, I said I would call a taxi and go home to collect the car and his wheelchair before returning. I am so grateful that I went when I did as I didn't have to watch the suffering when they came to do a lumbar puncture. This was quite a task as it wasn't possible for Mark to get into the correct position, and so they ended up putting him across a bedside table, and from all accounts, it really wasn't very nice.

By the time I returned, the pain in his head was starting to ease, and he was settled down for the night, and so I went back home. I had never been alone in the house, and I couldn't bring myself to sleep in our bedroom and so took a photograph of Mark with me and settled into bed in the spare room. I had been told that I could go back to the hospital for visiting at 2 pm the next day, and so I had put my suit ready for work the next morning as I planned to go in and occupy myself until visiting hours.

When I awoke the next day, to get ready for work, I knew I couldn't face going in because I was so anxious and so phoned the hospital to see if I could go in early to be with Mark. They agreed that I could, and I phoned college to explain what had happened. They were fantastic and very understanding, and so off I went to visit Mark at the hospital, still worrying about what was going to happen.

When I arrived at the hospital ward, where I had left him the previous night, I suddenly started to panic again when I realised he wasn't there. All sorts of thoughts went through my mind until a nurse came to tell me that he had been moved to another ward.

The ward he had been moved to was at the far end of the hospital, and my feet were killing me by the time I reached it. When I got to him, I again suggested that he let me phone his dad to let him know what had happened. He still didn't want me to call him, and the nurse explained that this ward was where patients were transferred to when they were going to be discharged.

Mark insisted that we wait until he was back home to phone, but eventually, after using my powers of persuasion (or, as Mark would say, 'nagging'), I managed to convince him that I should call and let his dad know what had happened. I also rang and told my parents. Mark's dad said he and Kathy would travel up the next morning from home, which is three hours south of where we live, and I was very glad to hear that. The next morning, I went to the hospital, and Mark's parents had agreed that they would meet me there.

Whilst I was on the ward with Mark, the consultant came on his rounds and confirmed, having run some tests, that it was most likely a virus that had triggered a migraine. Mark still had the pain and had been on liquid morphine every hour to help. Having been given the all-clear to be discharged from the hospital, we only had to wait for his medication to be sorted, and we would leave for home. I contacted his parents with the good news, and they were due to be with us within the next hour, and so I told them the ward to come to.

Mark, still with his pain, was apprehensive about leaving the hospital as he was told he would not be able to take morphine with him and he would need to have an alternative for the pain. His lunch arrived, and then as he was going to the loo, his pain worsened yet again and he was in agony. One of the nurses immediately came to him, and another bleeped the consultant to rush back. An emergency team arrived, and once again, he was back on the morphine intravenously. Eventually, a consultant came, and upon examining Mark and seeing what pain he was in, the consultant decided that he would stay in the hospital and would be sent to yet another ward. Just as he was about to be moved, his parents arrived, and I just broke down and sobbed — his dad was here now so I didn't need to be brave any longer!

We settled Mark in and then went home without him. We decided to go to a nearby restaurant that Mark and I visited on a regular basis. They asked how he was doing, and they were very surprised when all I could manage was a prawn cocktail because usually I would manage to devour three courses!

Mark would remain in the hospital for a further week under observation, and he was put back on liquid morphine, which was usually administered every four hours, but he needed it every hour to try and keep the severe pain under control. The ward he was in was a 'mixed' ward with a nurses' station in the middle. Whilst it was a very worrying time, we did have some funny moments that we will always remember. On one occasion, during the night, Mark told me that he thought he was hallucinating with the drugs: An elderly gentleman with a bald head, one eye, and severe limp came towards him and gave him some medication to take.

On another occasion, again during the night, a young female nurse came to Mark's aid. She had thought she was at a woman's bedside who wanted assistance to remove a bedpan. She gasped when she realised, while putting her hands under the bed sheet to remove the bedpan, that she was at the wrong bed and Mark wasn't the woman she should have gone to! Even funnier was that she quickly ran away, without so much as an apology, but she waited to meet me the next day and apologised to me instead!

Then there were two stories about the same elderly lady from the women's bay. First, she came and told Mark that he was in her bed and started taking off her clothes. Luckily for Mark, the nurse spotted what was happening and came to escort her back to her own bed. The second time, this lady came to see Mark and started searching for her hand cream, which she was convinced was in his bed, and so she kept grabbing his feet whilst looking for it.

Mark was eventually released from the hospital one Saturday afternoon and would be home for us to celebrate our wedding anniversary. By the Sunday morning, he was in severe pain again, and so I had to call out the emergency doctor who gave me a prescription for liquid morphine, and I rushed at speed to the chemist so that I wouldn't be gone too long as I didn't like leaving him whilst he was so ill.

On my return, I gave him the prescribed measure of liquid morphine and then hid the bottle out of his sight as I couldn't let him have any more for four hours. He had been so used to being given the liquid morphine every hour and made me feel really bad each time I had to refuse him. His headache lasted for nine more weeks before he would be able to finally go back to work.

By the time I went back to work, I hadn't been able to do the preparation that was necessary for me to deliver the Subject Learning Coach programme, and as though it was meant to be, the QIA was replaced by the Learning and Skills Improvement Service (LSIS), and I was invited to attend another residential programme to become an advanced learning coach. I explained that I had already been through the programme, and they informed me that this would be more in-depth and would introduce me to even more models. I am a big believer in 'what will be, will be', and this was an opportunity for me to revisit what I had been planning to do, and so I accepted.

I was on the 'pilot' cohort, and what followed was so stressful for me, but it would reap so many rewards and be perhaps the biggest learning experience I have ever had.

After signing up, I received an email instructing me to log on to a website and take the quiz. I was given the email address of my 'e-tutor', and so as I wasn't quite sure if I was on the right track, I decided to email him. To my horror, I received an 'out of office' reply informing me that he was away from his desk for the next two weeks. As I would be going on holiday myself at about the time he would be available, I started to panic somewhat.

I had to overcome my worries and do what I hoped would be right. As it was part of my job, I spent some of my time at work actually going into chat rooms — why then did I feel that I was being naughty whenever anyone came into my office?

I also spent my holiday in Spain using the Internet to do some of my work to prepare for the residential soon after I returned home. On arriving for the first day of the residential, I was greeted by a familiar face — it was the facilitator who had taken us for the previous ALC course. I was also delighted to learn, as he introduced me to a lady who would become my mentor on the ALC programme, that I was the first participant to achieve the ALC status with the QIA.

As we all sat down in readiness for the beginning of the event, I was scanning the room for familiar faces. One of the benefits of undertaking the pre-event quiz was that I was getting to know the other participants. In particular, I remember the 'Stig' — one of the participants had used the photograph of the 'Stig' from the television programme 'Top Gear'. I challenged myself to identify who it was before approaching he or she to ask if I had guessed correctly.

A question was thrown out to the group to ask how we had felt when completing the pre-event tasks. To my surprise, I wasn't the only person who had been in a panic, lacking confidence, and looking for reassurance that I had done everything correctly.

On reflection, as I mentioned earlier, this would be another great learning experience — I had found my way around the website and had been introduced to the other participants (and knew who to avoid at the residential)! Although I had lacked confidence that I was doing everything right initially, I realised that because of how I had felt I would be able to empathise with my students. This was a deeper learning experience, and I had learnt more than during any other lessons. Because of this, I had learnt far more than I would have if just being shown around the website and given the information (shallow learning). I had also realised that I should have more self-confidence and do what I think is right as if it wasn't someone would soon let me know!

The next day we were informed that we would have to produce a professional project. When would I find the time? My mentor came to see me back at college, and we discussed my outline for the professional project, which she agreed would be suitable. Sure enough, I found the time and managed to successfully gain accreditation.

Chapter 7

Changes

Changes is the title of one of David Bowie's records. I just have to include him in my book as he is one of my heroes and, as an agent of change and being flexible, I thought the chapter title was appropriate. I must also mention, with my OCD (obsessive compulsion disorder), that it is pronounced Bowie as in bow tie and not Bowie as in bow wow!

Ofsted visited us once again, and we were ready. I had been working hard with staff members across college to raise the standards in teaching and learning. There had been several changes in management, and the current manager had only been there for such a short period of time. Therefore, I was best placed to act as the ambassador for teaching and learning and put together an evidence file.

This time we achieved 'good' for all teaching and learning, and I was proud to have played my part, including being responsible for the whole of our department. Soon after this, we started to go through a restructure.

My very good friend Dawn was made vice-principal, and I was absolutely delighted. This meant that she was now over both departments for teaching and learning — one for youngsters on programme, ages sixteen to twenty-five, and the department, where I worked, for adults re-training to go back into employment.

She supported me immediately, allowing me time to do my team leader duties. This meant that instead of having a tutor group of my own, I shared my colleague's tutor group, and so I spent time in the class for two days a week when she wasn't in, being part-time, and then I had three days each week to carry out my team leader duties and include training, mentoring, and coaching others.

She was also pleased that I joined the Observations team as she knew that I had many years of experience in grading sessions. I carried on as a mentor and coach and supported and developed some of our staff in teacher training. I will be forever in Dawn's debt for her vision and support.

We continue to work well together to this day and have nothing but respect for one another, even though she would eventually move on to become the principal of another college. We now work together as board members of the Karten Network (see www.karten-network.org.uk for further information).

Did I mention that as part of our role, as directors on the Karten Network board, we meet up in London for board meetings, and there just happens to be a lovely cake shop in the train station when we are waiting for our train home?

Dawn's portion of yummy chocolate cake.

My job was going well, and with some of my time being taken outside the classroom, I was able to give more time to the Subject Learning Coach programme and the network meetings as well as share my knowledge and skills with my colleagues in college.

I was also given permission to become a Subject Learning Coach network facilitator. This was a paid role through an educational organisation. I was given the opportunity to gain even more skills whilst the money came into college to help cover my absences when going off for planning and delivery days.

One of the things I had never managed to do before was to feel comfortable to work with planned sessions and resources that had been created by someone else. I always found it easiest to produce my own schemes of work, lesson plans, and resources as I then knew what I expected from the students.

To begin with, I was asked to attend a 3-day planning event, and wow what a fantastic experience that was! I was in a room with about thirty consultants and another couple of participants who had also been asked to join as Subject Learning Coach network facilitators. The plan was obvious to me, at this stage, that what they wanted to achieve was organisations learning techniques to be able to eventually enable colleges to become centres of excellence to cascade good practice to other organisations.

We were initially welcomed and given an outline of the one-day Subject Learning Coach network meeting that we would be delivering. It was to consist of a starter activity which needed to be something active, and the good thing about this was that if participants arrived early, they would have something to occupy them until the day got underway. This would provide an opportunity for participants to mix and learn at the same time. It would also give me the opportunity to assess their knowledge and experience.

Some participants, like me, didn't need anything to occupy them as I am always straight in to introduce myself to others and find out something about them. Believe it or not, I used to be a shy and quiet person, but those friends and family who know me well know that I really am very extrovert these days. The day's network meeting would then be introduced and objectives for the session given. Then there would be a number of activities, around different topics, to actively engage the participants and enable assessment of learning to take place. The assessment of learning would take place through a series of fun activities such as quizzes and no mention of tests whatsoever!

We were then put into small groups, each one with the responsibility of planning a part of the day. My group were going to be responsible for the first activity around a theme. We got to work and had been informed that all groups were to meet up at 3 pm that day to each deliver their part of the session. We all did this and received feedback from the other groups, which let us know what they thought was good and what they thought needed to be improved. The idea we had come up with was found to be good in parts, but one of the quizzes we had demonstrated needed changing. We worked into the early evening to try and come up with alternatives and finally agreed that we would go for dinner and try and reflect throughout the rest of the evening and get together the following morning to make a decision about which quiz to use. The pressure on us was very intense, and I was exhausted but grateful for the knowledge that I was really learning here as to how to become a professional in the delivery of learning programmes in a new role.

I soon dropped off to sleep after eating a three-course meal, washed down with a glass or two of red wine. The strange thing was that at about four o'clock in the morning, I woke up with an idea for an activity we might be able to use. I grabbed a piece of paper and a pen and made a note. Then, as if by magic, I dropped back off into a restful sleep. It was an early start the next morning, and I was up at 6 am in the shower and dressed ready to tackle a traditional, full English breakfast. This would set me up for the day, well at least until lunchtime came and then the evening meal, and something told me that I would need to go on a diet after the three days of event planning!

We met as a small group, and I put forward my suggestion that had come to me at four o'clock that morning. It was agreed that we would go with it — I can't remember exactly what it was, but an example would be to produce a quiz for participants to work through in pairs. It would ask them to use the Subject Learning Coach website to find out some information about coaching skills using the GROW model. This would be a deep learning opportunity for participants rather than just being shown where to find it and an exposition being given about how it works (shallow learning).

We quickly put it together in the form of a handout, and then after the morning break when all the groups came together, we gave them the quiz to have a go at. As I stood back and watched, I saw pairs of consultants having fun together and identifying the key parts of the GROW model. We asked everyone to tell us something about the GROW model and, after a short time, we came to an agreement of what the GROW stands for and how it works. Basically, the GROW is as follows:

G = What is your **goal**?

R = What is the **reality**? What is stopping you from achieving your goal?

O = What are the **options/opportunities**? What can you do? What else can you do? What else can you do? What else can you do? (This same question is repeated in order to help focus not just on one option but several).

W = What **will** you do? What will you do first and when by?

Take a few minutes at this point and think of something you want to achieve or an issue you want to resolve maybe. Answer these questions and see just how it helps. This gives you some quality time to think about something and think about several options, not just one, that you could consider. You should then decide what you will do first of all and by when. Most importantly, use the SMART model when doing this, ie, make your targets specific, measurable, appropriate, realistic, and timely. (There can be a slight variation on a theme here, ie, different words used. However, the core message remains the same).

An example of this could be when I bought a new car which was the same make as my previous one, I thought I would know exactly what I needed to know in order to drive the car safely. The goal was therefore that I wanted to drive my new car safely so as not to get a dent in it. The reality was, however, that when I couldn't see clearly through my wing mirrors, I needed to reposition them. I immediately found the button to select the left or right wing mirror. However, it was slightly different to the electric controls on my old car, and I couldn't figure out how to reposition them. This was the reality. What were my options then? My first thought was to ring my husband and ask him! Then, as with the GROW model, I didn't rush in with my first idea (this would be an example of shallow learning if I was just told), but I thought about what else I could do. I took a few minutes and came up with a second idea, which was that I could ring the garage — only joking as this would also be shallow learning because they would most likely think, 'Typical women drivers!' What else could I do then? I could look in the manual that came with the car, or I could go on to the Internet and have a look at information there. I decided to take the manual with me and find the answer there hopefully. This would be the 'W'—what will you do? It should be SMART, so I was specific — that I would take the manual in the house with me. It would be measurable if I could find out how to reposition my wing mirrors. It was an appropriate and realistic task to undertake, and I made a decision to do it as my first job when I got home, with a cup of tea. I had managed to make my decision using a SMART goal. What then is the benefit of deeper learning over shallow learning? With the shallow learning option, one question to my husband, one answer. However, if I find out for myself by looking in the manual, I am more likely to remember what I need to do, and at the same time, by looking in the manual, I may find out some additional information.

Our colleagues all agreed that our activity worked very well, and it was approved for our part of the session planned. For the rest of that day, we added a few adjustments to our handout, and then we were good to go. The final day of the three was used for all the groups to demonstrate their activities, and so by the end, we all knew what we would have to do to deliver a standardised programme throughout the country. I had learnt so much and was exhausted as well as overweight by the end of the three days.

I was contacted about supporting the consultants with facilitating the Subject Learning Coach network meetings in several regions of the country. I would be working with one of the consultants whom I knew very well as she had facilitated many previous network meetings that I had attended. The first venue was in Northampton—I recall the parking fine. After a day at work, I jumped in the hire car to travel to Northampton, where I met Chris, whom I would be working with.

As she lived near the venue, she took me to a local restaurant, where we could relax with a glass of wine and some good food whilst planning details for the following day's session. I had offered to drive and so realised that I wouldn't be able to have a nice glass of Rioja after all. However, this was probably a good idea as I wanted to be well prepared for the next day, without a headache.

I parked the car and went to the meter to obtain a ticket, which I put on the window screen. What a shock when we returned to the car after such a lovely evening – I had a parking ticket with a note saying that my ticket was not displayed clearly, and so I was fined! In over thirty years of driving, I had never received any parking tickets. I had to admit I was in the wrong as when I looked at the window screen, the ticket was difficult to read through the tinted glass. The good news was that I wrote to the authority to ask for consideration regarding the fine as I had paid to park and enclosed the ticket as proof and it was only because it was a hire car that I hadn't realised the ticket could not be seen where I had placed it. I received a letter back to confirm that they would drop the charge on this occasion, but it did not mean that if a similar situation arose in the future, that I would be looked on so favourably.

The actual event went very well and I really enjoyed the experience. I couldn't possibly believe I could still be learning so much from this development opportunity, but once again, I was like a sponge soaking up water. The next event which I was scheduled to facilitate was in Manchester, a city I knew well as I have visited family members on many occasions. I met up with Sharon for a meal, and this time, as the car was parked up for the evening, I enjoyed a nice glass of Rioja too. I was starting to realise the full extent of involvement with each session facilitated. The fact that I was already working full-time in college and was then driving to the venue to have an evening of preparation and discussion followed by a full day of facilitation and then driving back home was making life fun but very hectic!

Back at work, as part of the restructure programme, the team leader positions were made obsolete, and I applied for two posts, one as a tutor and the other as a manager. It was a difficult time and, just before the holidays, I learned that I had been successful in securing the role of tutor but had not been successful in getting the role of manager. I wasn't worried about not getting the manager's job as it would be very much an administration role, and my passion was for making learning fun.

The vice-principal knew me well and when she called me into her office to tell me that I hadn't been successful in securing the manager's job, she said that the reason for this was that she knew it would make me ill. As a very caring person, I always put others' needs before my own and this can result in my getting stressed when I have tight deadlines to meet. She said that I would always have a role at Portland as a tutor but she wanted me to follow another direction as she had seen how much I was enjoying my work as a coach and how I was bringing back to college lots of good practices and sharing them with the staff to continually improve teaching and learning.

I had also, as part of the Advanced Learning Coach programme, learnt about influencing strategies and round-table building (the latter being about choosing who I wanted to work with) and I was putting these models into practice in order to make my dreams happen. I would recommend that you research both influencing strategies and round-table building, and you can find out where in the 'Further Reading' section.

There was an event coming up for managers, and we agreed that we would go together. I had been asked by the organisers to speak at the event to the managers to 'sell' the Subject Learning Coach programme. When talking to the managers about my experience of the Subject Learning Coach programme, I feel that I created a buzz and successfully helped to get more principals and quality managers from the FE sector on board with the programme. Not only that, but as we travelled home together, after the event, Dawn suggested that I find out about what possibilities I might have to develop my role further, for the good of the college. I took her at her word and began to investigate what opportunities there might be, including delivering some training to my colleagues and senior management, which I agreed with our quality manager.

Chapter 8

Consultancy

I had been in discussion with an educational organisation as I had seen jobs advertised for educational consultants. Surely, as others had thought, 'I was never that clever', I could not possibly become an educational consultant – right? Wrong – as I went on to discover.

I had spoken to some of my contacts and my vice-principal and decided to apply to become an educational consultant delivering programmes on behalf of LSIS. I put together an up to date CV, and although this was something I helped students to do on a daily basis, when it came to doing my own, I really struggled. Finally, I had prepared a CV and wrote a covering letter of application to accompany it.

When I opened the post a few days later, I could hardly believe my luck as I had been invited to attend an interview day. It just so happened that the date they wanted me to attend was right in the middle of my summer holiday fortnight, which I would be spending in Bournemouth to have some time by the coast and visit family at the same time. I was in a dilemma as I always said to my students that if they get an interview, they really need to attend it and not try to rearrange it because this could show that they didn't want the job bad enough. What should I do?

I used the GROW model to look at my options and how to ensure I didn't seem that I wasn't interested enough. I eventually contacted them to say I would be delighted to attend the interview and, in conversation, I mentioned I would be travelling back from my holiday to attend. On hearing this, the lady at the other end of the phone told me that apart from the date they had offered me, there was another date and they would be happy to swap if it helped. I agreed to change to the new date and told them how grateful I was for their offer and flexibility.

The day arrived for the interviews, which took the form of a team activity, an individual activity, and a formal interview. I wondered if there might be any negativity from any of the other consultants because of the fact I had applied for the role whilst already having full-time employment. My vice-principal had also mentioned that the rates paid to me as a Subject Learning Coach Network facilitator wasn't really enough to make it worthwhile for the college to keep releasing me. As if it was meant to be, the pay was at a higher rate for consultancy, and therefore, I could be released by the college.

In addition, all the other consultants were really kind and supportive towards me. It felt really strange that, if I was successful, I could be working with the consultant who had facilitated my learning on the Advanced Learning Coach programmes and whom I admired for his enthusiasm and commitment to the programme. I even mentioned that I had chuckled when seeing a short video of him and a colleague talking about the programme – his colleague did most of the talking and at the end Geoff piped up, 'And then there is Boyatzis'. We did laugh. Others wouldn't understand as you had to be there and I knew from attending the programme with him just how passionate he was about Boyatzis. It is worth searching on the Internet to find out more about Boyatzis (as mentioned in chapter 6), and you might even come across the video of Geoff and his colleague.

The first activity we had to do in small groups was to take a resource and create a learning activity to introduce participants to it. This was reasonably straightforward as I had the experience of using this resource when working as a Subject Learning Coach Network facilitator. We then had to deliver to the other interviewees, ensuring that we all played an active part. After lunch, I was formally interviewed by two team members of the educational organisation, and in particular, they wanted to know what I knew about the Subject Learning Coach programme. My passion and knowledge shone through, and I felt that it went very well. Lastly, I was given a scenario based around the website and e-mentoring students. The scenario involved two students who were obviously unhappy with the support they were getting, and I had to explain how I would deal with this situation. I explained that I would use the 'chat room' to tell them both that I was sorry about how they felt and inform them that I would message them separately to try and resolve their issues. This way I was hoping to avoid them putting any more negative comments on the 'chat room' and make them feel supported at the same time.

I rushed into my vice-principal's office, waving my letter around as I had been successful and was taken on for a six-month contract to deliver network meetings and to work as an e-mentor for participants who would be joining cohorts for the Subject Learning Coach Professional Training Programme. I was officially an educational consultant, and I was invited to attend an induction day in Old Windsor.

Wouldn't you just know it — the day I was going to be travelling to Old Windsor for the induction day, we had Ofsted in yet again! As a specialist provision college, we received an annual inspection visit. I was asked to carry out a co-observation with the Ofsted inspector, which was fine as I was experienced in this field, having carried out co-observations with Ofsted before. However, when the meeting was held later in the morning for me to give my feedback and grade, I explained I had to leave early afternoon to catch a train for Old Windsor. Her words were, 'I will have your written observation report before you leave, won't I?'

I stopped myself from gasping and replied, 'Of course, you will.' Why do I get myself in these situations? I shut myself in the office with the quality manager sitting outside in the corridor to ensure that under no circumstances was I going to be disturbed. With a very tight deadline of only 25 minutes, I did it! Admittedly, it wasn't as good as it could have been, had I had more time, and I did have to shout the quality manager in on a couple of occasions because I couldn't think of the words I wanted to use as my mind kept going blank. I printed out and signed my observation report and passed it to the quality manager, before running to get my lift to the station.

I arrived in Old Windsor, very tired after an exhausting morning with Ofsted but really buzzing from all the excitement in my life at this time. How everything was happening for me was just amazing. I bumped into Geoff, who congratulated me on becoming a consultant. I was so very proud of myself and wanted to learn everything I could from the experience.

Then some other familiar faces appeared, and I settled in for an evening of chatter and reflected with my colleagues. It was time for bed, and I had planned to 'Skype' Mark to let him know that I had arrived safely and settled in as well as bore him with the details of my morning with Ofsted. He is such a good listener even though I often waffle on! On my way back to the room, I phoned Mark to let him know I would set up my laptop to contact him. It was such a very long walk to my room, and one of my colleagues had already asked to be moved as the corridors were long and quiet, so she felt that it wasn't really safe for a woman on her own. At least I was on the phone to Mark which made me feel safe and as I eventually arrived at my room after what felt like the distance of a marathon, I couldn't get my key card to work and so, you guessed it, I had to walk all the way back to reception!

What made matters even worse was that when I finally got into my room and set up the laptop, I couldn't get any connection to use Skype. Once again, I took that long journey to reception so I could get a better connection on the phone to let Mark know I couldn't use Skype. What a night!

One of the things we had been asked to do for the induction was to bring along a shoe box with three things in that represented us as an individual suitable for the consultancy. I had put in a small bottle of champagne (which I would then be able to drink of course), and this represented that I like quality items. Another item I put in was a mirror, and the third a box of Quality Street. I said that the mirror represented me as a good reflector and that the box of Quality Street represented my passion for sharing with others, and in addition, I said that I was very resourceful as by drinking the champagne and sharing the Quality Street with everyone there, I wouldn't have to carry them back home with me!

I received details relating to what venues I would be working in, including dates, and it was confirmed that I would get an email about who I would be mentoring in due course.

One Thursday, during the winter months, I was having a hire car dropped off for me at college, and I would be going to Burton on the Friday, and then on the following Monday, I was to go to Cambridge.

The weekend before, in preparation for my trips, we had purchased a satellite navigation system and tried it out when we travelled to Essex to visit Mark's family. We had booked into a hotel which had wheelchair access, and we had stayed there previously. We had already experienced severe weather conditions which had trapped us in our bungalow for seven days before help came to dig us out as the snow had drifted up the drive and was about two to three feet in depth. Now, we were attempting to drive to Essex and, as we got closer, big snowflakes started to fall.

We pulled up at the hotel which has several steps up to the reception and an outside lift to enable wheelchair users to gain access. We are familiar with these types of lift and I was surprised that I couldn't find the controls to activate it. I climbed the slippery steps up to reception and was greeted by a young receptionist with a lovely smile. She explained that people had been misusing the lift and so they kept the controls behind reception and she would come out and operate it when we were ready.

I returned to Mark in the car, and he got out and put his jacket on as I was nagging at him for not wanting to wear it. He said it was worth wearing it to stop my nagging. The temperature was dropping as he got into the lift, and by this time, the young receptionist had appeared with the controls.

I had decided that rather than travelling in the lift with him, I would use the steps and carry the bags. Suddenly, there was a screeching noise coming from the lift, and then it stopped. It wouldn't move up, and it wouldn't move down. The motor had frozen solid. The smile on the young receptionist's face disappeared and instead there was a look of panic setting in fast. She tried switching the electric off and back on again for a few moments, but that didn't work.

She asked us to wait, and she would be back as quickly as possible to get the problem sorted. After only a few minutes, she returned and informed us that help was on the way. She asked if we would like a hot cup of coffee while we waited, and I replied that I would prefer a brandy, and I got one. Then she told us that they had called the fire brigade and she kept apologising for such an inconvenience. She had still continued to try and get the lift moving, but it just wasn't going to happen. Suddenly, we heard sirens, and then the fire brigade were approaching with the blue lights flashing.

At that very moment, the lift started to work, and the receptionist's look of panic was then replaced with a blush of embarrassment. It did stop again, and we had a fire crew ready to use a fireman's lift. Luckily for us they carried out the rescue and it was decided to use the goods lift at the back of the building. Once inside the building, they called the lift to take them up to reception. As the doors opened and they entered the lift, to their surprise, they found a couple using the lift for other things and not for what it was intended. Mark found himself staring at the woman's open blouse and her lover! I will leave the rest to your imagination.

The receptionist was so apologetic about the whole episode, and I explained that I have a real love for red fire engines and blue flashing lights – not the firemen though. People always think that my love is really for the firemen however and so I then have to explain that my brother had been in the fire service, and so I had visited the fire station on many occasions when I worked nearby and he would give me a lift home. It really is the fire engine and blue lights that I love.

Now then, where was I? Oh yes, I was about to tell a story about the satellite navigation system and my trips to Burton and Cambridge. On the Friday morning, I was up early to travel to Burton and I got into the hire car and plugged my sat nav into the cigarette lighter. It was dark outside, and so I put the interior light on so as to be able to find the cigarette lighter. As I plugged in the sat nav, I heard a 'pop' and saw a blue flash. I was a little startled, and, as I knew my way to Burton, along the A38, I decided I would drive without using the sat nav because I wasn't sure how much battery power it had and didn't want to try and plug it in a second time until I could see better. When I arrived in Burton, I put it on to get me to the venue.

I arrived in good time and settled in for a day's session. During the day, I had a chance to discuss ideas for resources and as always went home with lots more ideas and feeling creative. When I came out of the meeting, it was still light, and so I was able to investigate what the problem with the cigarette lighter was. To my surprise, there was a glass fuse in it which I had broken when trying to plug in the sat nav. I removed it and thought no more about it.

The following Monday, I was travelling to Cambridge in preparation for facilitating a network meeting but first of all decided to go into work to check that my students were OK, and I eventually left work at around 3 pm. I plugged in the sat nav and because I had just started to trust it to replace my map book, I hadn't bothered to work out the route but did put my map book in the car should I need it for any reason.

I was doing really well and had a good 'trouble-free' journey that was until I was just about to leave the motorway. Suddenly, I heard the sat nav announce that it had run out of battery power, and it then shut down! I learnt after all not to rely on the sat nav entirely as I had to exit the motorway and pull into a lay-by. I realised that when the glass fuse had been smashed by my putting the sat nav connection in the cigarette lighter, it must have also blown its fuse. It was dark by this time, and I couldn't see the map very easily. I continued my journey until I reached a supermarket and pulled into the car park.

A smartly dressed, elderly gentleman was walking my way, and so I stopped him to ask if he could help with directions to the Moller Centre, Churchill College, University of Cambridge. He said he hadn't heard of it but the road it was on was not too far away. I finally reached my destination thankfully and met up with some of the other consultants who were also facilitating at the event.

It was a very good event and I received positive feedback from the participants. I also had comments from other consultants that my group were the noisy ones. Well, I do like to ensure that the participants have fun and we were laughing rather loudly!

On another occasion, I facilitated an event at Birmingham Motor Museum, which was an added bonus as I do like fast cars.

Another part of my consultancy was to mentor and coach participants on the Subject Learning Coach Professional Training Programme, and I really enjoyed the opportunity to support and advise them through the 'chat room' and email via the Subject Learning Coach website – to find out more go to *http://tlp.excellencegateway.org.uk/tlp/slc/*. Having followed this route myself, I felt that I could encourage them to do what I had and just how amazing and beneficial I had found the programme and network meetings.

Chapter 9

Funding for Action Research

During the period when I was employed as a consultant, I also applied for funding in order to carry out some action research. I believe that action research is an excellent opportunity to improve teaching and learning, and I agree with a statement by Jean McNiff (2002): 'Action research involves a systematic and cyclical method of planning, taking action, observing, evaluating (including self-evaluation) and critical reflecting prior to planning the next cycle'.

I was able to look at current practices and identify and put actions in place to improve my sessions. We also introduced a self-evaluation form for teaching staff to complete following formal observations.

The funding meant that a colleague was able to cover my usual teaching sessions whilst I delivered the SLC PTP. We were also funded for the costs of room hire, and resources could be purchased as necessary.

The first application I put in was approved, and I was able to deliver the Subject Learning Coach Professional Training Programme to a small group of teachers, some from my college, a teacher from a sixth form of a local school, and others from another further education college. I felt this was important because this meant that good practices could be shared across organisations.

When I undertook the programme, it included several sessions, including residentials, but over a period of time, the programme had been cut until eventually, it was a 2-day programme, which I would imagine was due to cuts in funding available. It is my belief that this would impact on the quality of the programme as with the residential sessions in particular, much was gained such as networking with like-minded people and sharing ideas for resources and effective methods for learning.

Therefore, when I planned for delivering the programme, I chose to deliver it over five days, which would be spaced out and therefore give the participants a chance to undertake some action research and produce resources and an assignment before starting on a new topic.

I remember the first session: I had prepared a pre-event task which was based on finding out some information on the programme they would be involved in, and this encouraged them to experience 'deeper learning' by having to explore the website for the Subject Learning Coach Programme independently. I remember how I had felt that first time I was exploring the website to undertake the quiz and how I wanted someone to tell me I was on the right track.

I had also prepared a starter task so that when people arrived for the session, they had something to do whilst waiting for everyone to arrive. I think it is a good idea to have a starter activity prepared so that if participants don't know each other, it can provide an activity where they have to speak to other participants and I can observe them. It also gives an opportunity for participants to experience 'deeper learning' rather than my telling them some information, which is an example of 'shallow learning'. Think about something you learned when you had a demonstration perhaps. Then think about something you had to find out about yourself, perhaps in a quiz. Whilst many people I have spoken to would have preferred to be shown and then 'have a go' themselves, they have confirmed that when they have had to find out something themselves, it has been easier to remember and they have found out more useful information also.

The main thing about the day's session was that it was very active. In other words, all learning that was taking place was by the participants working through quizzes and other activities such as piecing together a jigsaw to answer questions and using the Internet to find the right answers to other questions. Working in pairs, they would have a question to find the answer for and then give feedback to the rest of the group.

This meant that I only 'facilitated' the session whilst they did all the work. It did mean however that I had to spend longer in planning as it was essential to have good resources. I found it very difficult to begin with as I felt as though I wasn't teaching them anything, but in fact, they learnt so much more through this strategy, and I even found out things I wasn't aware of!

When I have previously mentioned 'emotional intelligence', one of the things to remember is that you should be able to laugh at yourself and make mistakes but learn from them. As we were preparing to take a break for some lunch, I used a technique called 'Columbo'. This is effective to keep participants or students on track by not mentioning that you want them to do something before break. As soon as the word 'break' is mentioned, you have lost their attention, and they begin gathering their things. Instead, as Detective Columbo would say, 'One more thing . . .' Using this technique keeps the students on task.

I then presented them with my bingo activity, which would allow me to assess that learning had taken place. There are websites available that are free to use in order to make bingo cards, but on this occasion, I had used it as a 'live work' activity for some of my students to produce them using Word. I had them laminated so that I could use them over and over, trying to be resourceful. The bingo activity went well, and one of the students shouted when she had a line. She had won a prize, and we carried on for a full house. Then came disaster for me, the Queen of Perfection — two participants both shouted 'house'.

There had been a mistake, well three actually:

> I realised that I had two bingo cards which were identical — whoops!
> I realised that if I wanted it doing right, I should perhaps do it!
> Finally, I learnt that I should test activities before spending a fortune to have laminating done!

Remember that you are allowed to make mistakes as long as you learn from them. Research suggests that you learn more when something goes wrong as long as you work with it and make changes as necessary and then try again. It might take three or four attempts, but hopefully, you will get it perfected.

As we had a full-day packed with learning activities and techniques that I would be modelling, I had produced a reflective log so that participants could make notes at regular intervals. Basically, the log was a Word table with the name of the activity or technique being modelled and space for making notes and planning how they could be used back in the classroom. This would act as a reminder of what had been covered in the session so that participants could reflect further.

After lunch, some time was given for the participants to reflect on what they had seen demonstrated and what they had engaged in. We then all came together and recapped on what the morning had included and how they felt it went. They were all very enthusiastic and full of praise, which was wonderful as I am very passionate about improving teaching and learning, and I wanted to cascade it to others.

One of the difficulties that I experienced when undertaking the professional training programme was a lack of time to use the Subject Learning Coach website, go to *http://tlp.excellencegateway.org.uk/tlp/ slc/* for further information and to make resources. Accordingly, I incorporated time during the session for pairs to explore the website and to identify resources to produce, and during following sessions, they were able to not only produce resources but also to trial them on the rest of the group. Having seen my bloomer with the bingo activity, they were comfortable in risk taking themselves rather than being preoccupied that they were going to make mistakes. They also gave good constructive feedback to each other and shared further ideas.

Another idea I used was a 'paper-plane' when asking participants to share an idea with the rest of the group. It was after lunch, and the participants were a little sluggish, so I gave them all a piece of A4 paper and asked them to write their idea or resource on it. Once they had done that, I encouraged them to make a paper-plane.

We then went outside, and I lined them up ready to throw their planes. The one which went the furthest won a prize. We did have a laugh, and we shared good practices and woke up ready to settle into more work.

To celebrate their achievements and development at the end of the programme, we all enjoyed a Christmas meal at a local restaurant, and even then I took along a jigsaw for them to do so I could assess their learning! Jigsaw makers can be found on the Internet, and you type in the questions and answers, and then a jigsaw is made for printing out and cutting up.

I am proud to have seen my first cohort of Subject Learning Coaches GROW and raise their own standards in the classroom and practise their coaching skills whilst supporting colleagues to improve their lessons too. I think I can conclude that this had been a very worthwhile action research project and I was able to produce a report and case study to demonstrate the effectiveness and positive outcomes.

Following the success of this action research project, I went on to apply for more funding and was again successful. This time, I wanted to carry out an action research project to use staff development opportunities as a way of sharing good practices in order to improve observation grades.

This research would involve my working with the vice-principal and quality manager to plan and deliver training to teaching staff, encouraging staff to share good practices and ideas for resources, through 'show and tell' sessions. I mentored staff new to teacher training, and as their confidence grew, I then used coaching techniques to help them to identify themselves how they could improve their sessions for the students to have an outstanding learning experience. I delivered additional training, for staff in teacher training, together with the quality manager. She had previously participated in the Subject Learning Coach Professional Training Programme that I had offered and so was familiar with the theories and active learning involved. One of the sessions we delivered was 'What makes an outstanding session' and we took in our mixing bowls and wooden spoons to make the session both active and fun. The staff had to sort a selection of activity cards with statements on into the appropriate mixing bowl, and we had one for each Ofsted grade, ie, outstanding, good, requires improvement, and inadequate.

As a result of this second piece of action research, we were able to raise the percentage of sessions being graded good or better.

The quality manager went on to become vice-principal at another college, so when she left, I gave her a 'leaving' present, which was based on the shoebox activity previously mentioned (see below).

The Shoebox Activity (in a bag as I didn't have a shoebox big enough)!

Emergency Survival Kit

This kit contains items to transform teaching and learning on the farm!

Farm animals game	to raise satisfactory teaching and learning to outstanding within the next three years
Set of seeds	to GROW your staff
Wine and sweets	to survive difficult staff
Sheep dog	to 'round up' your staff and students
Biscuits (Weight Watchers)	to support your principal
Warning	

Use these resources wisely with due care and attention. Remember Ofsted and age appropriateness!

Staff members were encouraged to take part in peer observations, in addition to formal observations and those undertaken for mentoring and coaching purposes, and this worked really well. After the staff were initially made aware of the work of Joyce and Showers, they were asked to carry out peer observations and report back to say whether they found them useful.

One colleague came to me to say she was disappointed at whom she had been paired up with as she felt he was usually quite negative and didn't listen. I explained that I needed someone to share good practices who was also patient and understanding and I knew I could rely on her. The result was fantastic – I was pleasantly surprised when she came to tell me that she had found the experience very rewarding, and she emailed other staff to encourage them to take part in the peer observations as it was very worthwhile. Not only had she given her colleague support and ideas, but she had also come away with valuable information and ideas to include in her sessions.

I was able to produce another case study and a report which evidenced that the action research I had undertaken improved observation grades. Also, all staff members were motivated and enthusiastic when attending events that I facilitated and during mentoring and coaching sessions.

Nowadays, when I walk down the corridor, I hear all the students having fun whilst learning! I would definitely recommend carrying out action research when you want to improve something.

I suddenly found myself in demand and was asked by other colleges if I would be willing to facilitate their staff development sessions. This was another fantastic opportunity for me to share good practices with teachers in other organisations whilst also taking away effective ideas and examples of resources. In fact, one college had been successful in their bid for an action research project, which actually included me as a resource!

Chapter 10

Conclusion

I have thoroughly enjoyed every moment of my journey and still have to pinch myself sometimes. I have learned so much, including developing quality resources and sessions that will engage learners to learn. I have used the ten pedagogies to vary sessions as follows:

Cooperative learning	Experiential learning
Multi-sensory learning	Learning conversations
Differentiation	Assessment for learning
Relating theory and practice	Embedding literacy, language and numeracy in sessions
Using e-learning and technology	Modelling

I have also used the models and protocols effectively to enhance sessions:

The GROW model for coaching	Boyatzis—model of intentional change
Joyce and Showers—peer observation	Johari window
Iceberg model	Emotional intelligence
Reflective models	Bloom's taxonomy
Modes of learning	Traits

Action learning sets	Strategies for facilitating group discussion
Appreciative enquiry	Using a think piece
Round-table building	Happy families
Questioning for understanding	Triads
Teaching squares	

(To find the ten Pedagogical activity cards and model and protocol cards, see details in the 'Further Reading' section. I would recommend that you try and use some which are out of your comfort zone — take a risk)!

I can't quite believe that I am where I am now — a successful teacher, with over twenty years experience of working with people who have a wide range of disabilities, being asked to mentor and coach others, working as a consultant, and finally writing a book about my journey.

In the future, I want to continue to share my experience, inspire others, and continue working with students who give me so much pleasure when I see all that they achieve. I will continue to carry out action research, coach others, and perhaps even write another book!

I am sure that my journey isn't over yet. Having been introduced to Gervase Phinn and my friendly Ofsted inspector, Nick Sanders, I may well think about applying to become an Ofsted inspector too.

An Ode to My Maths Teacher

My maths teacher showed me how not to teach
Because of him the exam was out of my reach
He told me more than once that I was not clever
To become a teacher I could never
If only I could tell him now
That as a matter of fact he taught me how
To help and guide my students to achieve
Whatever their dream they should believe
In my belly there is a fire
To make learning fun is my desire
And so dear maths teacher
I want you to know
I wasn't stupid and wanted to show
I have been successful along several paths
And by the way I achieved my maths!

Key to Ideas, Models, and Resources

Below I have listed some of the ideas, models and resources mentioned throughout the book to help you find them for reference purposes.

Demonstration	page 15
Assessment of learning	pages 15, 23,48,62,
Using real examples	pages 23, 28
Facilitator	page 27
SMART goals	pages 27, 64
Peer observations	pages 30, 84
Girl teaching her hamster to sing	page38
(this replaces the words Boy teaching his dog to whistle)	
Icebreakers and starter activities	page 41
Action learning sets	pages 42, 46
Active learning	pages 42, 48, 62, 80
Show and tell	page 42
Blockbusters activity	page 43
Post-it notes activity	page 44
Action research	pages 78, 83
Innovative resources	page 45
Independent learning	page 45
Subject Learning Coach Professional Training Programme	page 45
Models and protocols	pages 46, 86
Ten pedagogies	pages 46, 86
GROW model	pages 47, 86

Further Reading

There are a variety of text books, publications and websites where you can find out more information. Also, see the listings below.

www.karten-network.org.uk

books by author Gervase Phinn (Penguin)

Jean McNiff (2002) Standards Unit, Teaching and Learning Division (2005) Participant Guide Module 2, 44 Action research.

Joyce B and Showers, B (1996) The Evolution of Peer Coaching, Educational Leadership, 53 (6): 12-16.

Kotter, J (1996) Leading Change, Cambridge: Harvard Business School Press.

Standards Unit, Teaching and Learning Division (2005) Participant Guide Module 2, 43 The Kolb cycle of learning.

Whitmore, J (2003) Coaching for Performance—Growing People, Performance and Purpose. London: Nicholas Brealey.

www.excellencegateway.org.uk

www.lsis.org.uk

www.ofsted.gov.uk

www.nationalstemcentre.org.uk

https://www.gov.uk/government/organisations/
department-for-business-innovation-skills

About the Author

Having worked in administration and customer service roles for a period of ten years, Christine began her journey into teaching in 1987 and accepted her first full-time post with a college for people with disabilities in 1989 and is still there today. The range of disabilities is vast and includes cerebral palsy, epilepsy, autism, and associated learning difficulties.

Her role as a teacher has continually changed, over the years, to ensure that her students are being trained in relevant subjects to assist them in gaining employment, according to the needs of the job market, and developing life skills to be able to live more independently.

She has mentored other teachers to the highest standards, using innovative methods and creative resources over the last twenty years. She was also invited to work with City & Guilds to create a qualification for desktop publishing.

Following an Ofsted report in 2004, which recognised her for good practice, in 2005, Christine was invited to engage with a government initiative to improve the standards in teaching and learning.

As an advanced learning coach, she received funding to carry out action research, delivered the Subject Learning Coach Professional Training Programme to teachers in the FE sector, and worked as an educational consultant, facilitating a series of network meetings to teachers nationwide.

She was asked to become a director for the Karten Network, which encourages CTEC Centres to share good practices.

She has met people who have inspired her throughout her personal journey and wanted to write this book to inspire others to choose a career in teaching to engage learners and make learning fun!

She is humbled to work with incredible learners, with a wide range of physical disabilities and associated learning difficulties, and still loves her job as much today as she did over two decades ago.

Index

A

B

C

D